For His Glory

COLIN CHALMERS

⊙

ISBN-13: 9781983071744

⬛

This book is dedicated to my wife Jenni—
my partner in living to bring Him glory.

Contents

Introduction

God—
Life Interruption
or Exciting Adventure?

In all your ways submit to him.

PROVERBS 3:6

I have brought you glory on earth by
finishing the work you gave me to do.

JOHN 17:4

Rejoice in the Lord always.

PHILIPPIANS 4:4

Often when I think about faith or trust, I put the
focus on myself: *Am I trusting? Am I a hero of the
faith?* It's not always wrong to ask these questions,
but I don't want to miss the most important thing of
all: God desires glory. He wants to be honored; he
wants his due simply for being God.

My faith and trust in him are for his glory, not
mine. What a difference it makes when I stop trying
to be a "super Christian" in my own strength and

instead begin asking how I can glorify him. God knows best how to bring himself glory, so I want to submit myself to him, get to know him better, then act on what he says.

However, there's a warning I give myself: *Anything I do can be done for the wrong reasons.* Anxiety has been an issue for me my whole life, and it brings with it the temptation to serve God out of the fear that I won't please him, or that I might destroy my life. Maybe you also have things that push you to follow God from a motive other than love.

I want you and me to keep Jesus's example in mind. He modeled maintaining a relationship with the Father by taking time to be with him. He persevered in prayer until his heart was ready to follow, then he joyfully acted out his Father's will. Not that his every act necessarily felt joyful, but love and joy were at the core of his motivation.

Life with God is a win-win situation—we just can't help but be satisfied when he's glorified.

As you join me on this thirty-day journey, I believe you'll find that you were made to bring him glory. As you put your focus first on God, life becomes an exciting adventure.

So read on—and let your prayer be the same as mine: "Lord, be glorified through me!"

Day 1

Consider how the wild flowers grow.

LUKE 12:27

As I recently drove from Ventura to Santa Barbara, California, I looked at the hills and thought, "He owns the cattle on a thousand hills" (Psalm 50:10). I looked at the birds in the nearby trees and thought of Jesus saying how "not one falls to the ground without your heavenly Father knowing about it" (Matthew 10:29). I realized that each place I looked could spark a thought about God—reminding me of who he is and what he's doing.

What an amazing way for us to continually delight in God and be filled with his joy! I want to do this more and more. As I train myself to be continually reminded of him, my mind will be transformed and my life will bring him glory.

Jesus, while on earth you used everything around you to teach. You asked that we consider the wild flowers, and it's likely they were there right in front of you to look at. Work in me so that everything might

11

*remind me of you. Each and every
day from now on, may everything I
see spark a "God thought"—a
thought about the often unseen
reality we live in. Allow me to delight
in you in this way, to be continually
reminded of you, and to be
constantly sharing these reminders
with others. Transform my mind that
my life might bring you glory! Amen.*

Day 2

Not a single one of all the good
promises the Lord had given to the
family of Israel was left unfulfilled;
everything he had spoken came true.

JOSHUA 21:45, NLT

One of the most important things in our daily worship of God is remembering his track record. Specific events, blessings, or times of being saved from a bad situation must be remembered in order to trust God now and into the future.

One of the promises God has kept in my life is the promise to provide financially as I put his agenda first. I remember a time when I believed the Lord wanted me to give my perfectly good car to the Salvation Army as a donation. About a week before I was to donate it, the car had major engine trouble that would require virtually all the money in my bank account to fix. I had to choose at that point whether to simply donate the car immediately or to get it put back into working condition first. I believed the Lord wanted it donated in working condition, but I also saw how much money this would cost (for something that wouldn't directly benefit me). After much prayer and struggle I had the engine work done. The Lord did his part in providing everything I needed afterward through many random gifts and various jobs. I focused on doing what God wanted, and he took care of providing for the expense. Since then, in more than a decade of similar situations, his provision has never lapsed.

In the verse above from the book of Joshua, the people of Israel remembered that God had not only done great things but had also promised these things beforehand. God keeps his promises. Not just some, but *all* of them.

He'll continue to keep his promises to us—we can trust in him even when it looks like we're giving up everything. God knows our needs better than we do, and he is powerful to work in us and around us for his glory.

Father, not a single one of the promises you made to Israel went unfulfilled. You are the faithful God who's willing to make great promises. Help me remember your promises and your faithful acts as I worship daily through what I do. You alone know all my needs, love me fully, and hear me at all times. You've saved me in the midst of impossible situations and have given me your hope, peace, and encouragement. You've changed my attitude and perspective countless times. You've made me wait for something when that's best for me and will bring you more glory. There's no one else like you—you have all power, yet you still love me deeply. There's no promise you've left unfilled, and today I remember again all that you've done in my life and in the lives of others around me. You cannot help but glorify yourself, God, and I delight in you!

Day 3

Do not be like the horse or the mule,
which have no understanding but must
be controlled by bit and bridle or they
will not come to you.

PSALM 32:9

Yet not what I will, but what you will.

MARK 14:36

Jesus makes it clear, when he prays in the garden before his arrest, that we have a will that isn't always the same as God's.

Our minds and desires don't always agree with God's desires. We must use our minds to choose to submit to God. He wants us to come to him willingly and ask what he wants, instead of our needing to be forced to follow (like a stubborn horse or mule).

Does God have plans for our lives? It would seem so. Paul wrote that "we are God's handiwork, created in Christ Jesus to do good works, which God prepared in advance for us to do" (Ephesians 2:10). And Paul said this to Archippus: "See to it that you complete the ministry you have

16

received in the Lord" (Colossians 4:17). Apparently Archippus was able to delay or put aside the work specifically given to him; Paul, being part of this man's community in Christ, exhorted him to finish.

We also are encouraged to finish—or to begin! God plans to bring himself glory through our lives.

Father, may I always come to you willingly with a sincere heart of desire. I don't seek complete independence from you, but rather a deep relationship of love. I know you've given me a mind—help me use it to choose you. Not my will but yours be done in everything. I choose to submit myself to you, and I want to know the things you've planned— since before the creation of the world—for me to do. Help me complete the work given to me in your name. Surround me with people who'll encourage me, who'll help me be built up in you, and who'll work alongside me. As you do all this, use me to encourage others as well. Bring yourself great glory through my life, just as you desire to do!

Day 4

For God is working in you, giving you
the desire and the power to do what
pleases him.

PHILIPPIANS 2:13, NLT

If living your whole life to please God doesn't
sound exciting yet, it may soon. Paul says in
Philippians 2:13 that God is giving us not only the
ability to do what pleases him but the desire as well.
This is not from ourselves; rather, it's God making
us to be like himself – to want what he wants. We
get to have joy and bring him glory at the same
time!

Years ago, before I was married, I began to pray
for God to help me put him first in everything. God
was giving me the desire to have an "undivided
heart" for him.

As soon as I began praying this, God began
pointing out other "gods" in my life. One of the
things taking God's place was my stuff—my
material possessions. I sensed that he was inviting
and challenging me to get rid of everything I
owned.

I don't think everyone needs to physically give up all their possessions, but God was showing me that my things had become more important to me than him. The test: When asked by him to get rid of my stuff, could I do it or not? For a whole year—almost two—I couldn't do it. I would try, but couldn't even throw one thing away. Finally, I told God I couldn't do it and that he would have to somehow give me the ability if it was to happen.

God did give me the ability—he cleared my internal opposition to his will and I began to desire what he desired. Then the next challenge came: The opposition of others. Many people either didn't understand or were challenged by what I was doing. Some people seemed partially supportive: "Don't get rid of your stereo!" Or, "God called you to play music, so it's crazy to get rid of your guitars." Persevering through the opposition would have been much more difficult had not God at the same time been giving me such a passion to obey him. I was filled with joy and a great sense of freedom.

I got rid of almost everything, then sensed that God was saying: "Stop, that's enough." It seems I'd finished just in time, because a few weeks later I got married and moved—requiring all my possessions along with unexpected but wonderful wedding gifts to fit into a small trailer borrowed from a friend. Through it all, God had worked on my heart and increased my overall enjoyment of him.

May he get the praise and glory for hearing our prayers and for giving us the desire and power to do what pleases him.

> *Lord, continue to give me the desire and power to do what pleases you. I want to fully enjoy you, and I look forward to being fulfilled as you gain great glory from being seen at work in my life.*

Day 5

Since you have been raised to new life
with Christ, set your sights on the
realities of heaven, where Christ sits in
the place of honor at God's right hand.

COLOSSIANS 3:1, NLT

We now have a life that's very different from the
life we had before following Christ. We have new
goals related to a new mission and new reasons for
living. In fact, our life is lived no longer for
ourselves but for others. This doesn't mean we
don't take proper care of ourselves—to successfully
take care of others, we have to be in the best shape
possible. Therefore even taking care of ourselves
has a new motivation, now that we're with Christ.

So why look at the realities of heaven? When
we know that God is really there, that Christ is
really alive, and that we have a coming inheritance
better than anything we've ever known, we can
spend our lives for his kingdom and not miss out on
any of his blessings now or later. We become
effective in our ministry to others. We become
focused—knowing what really matters.
Additionally, we have peace, because each moment

of every day Jesus is in heaven and has everything under control. Where he is, there's no turmoil or chaos. Anxiety melts when faced with the realities of heaven.

We make decisions differently than people who live without Christ, because we make them in light of a different reality. Without looking to the realities of heaven, we have only the realities of earth—the earth we knew well in our life without Christ. So what's different about you now? Today, how will you make decisions differently from how you made them before you knew the Lord? Will you act out of a place of peace even as chaos surrounds you?

If people don't understand why we do what we do, it's because they don't see the realities of heaven. However, many will see God at work in us and through us, and he will gain glory.

Father, help me live knowing that my life is entirely new. Set my sights on the realities of heaven. Bring me again and again to the place where your mission—grounded in love—is everything for me. Bring me to the place where I can love others sacrificially, knowing that I'm gaining everything that's really worth being gained. May you be more real to me each moment than the circumstances I see around me. May my feelings, thoughts, and actions all reflect your realities—for your glory.

Day 6

The Pharisee stood by himself and
prayed: "God, I thank you that I am not
like other people—robbers, evildoers,
adulterers—or even like this tax
collector."

LUKE 18:11

How often we compare ourselves to other people
instead of to Christ. We might tell the officer who
pulls us over, "I was just following the pace of
traffic; some of the cars ahead of me were going
even faster." Still, things look different if the officer
simply asks: "Were you or were you not going
fifteen miles per hour over the speed limit?"

The Lord has often made me aware of times
where I felt good about myself because I was doing
good things. Sometimes I've thought that I'm doing
more good things than other people are. Even if that
were true (it probably isn't), I'm not made good by
the good things I do. I must see myself as God sees
me, and remember who it is that makes me good.

We must not color our perception of God and
his justice by looking at how our lives measure in
comparison to others. The truth is that we all fall

terribly short of God's standards, and so we need Christ to save us. We bring God great glory when we remember where we would really stand without him, and how much he has done for us.

God, save me from comparing myself with others to determine how good I am. Father, if I must compare or measure myself, let me compare myself to Christ. Surely this will kill my sinful pride and remind me of how much I need you. And please, Lord, don't let me color my perception of who you are by looking at myself as good. I am not the standard; you are. Help me see Jesus, because he reveals who you really are—a God who is good and just. And while I have no way to make myself good, you still see me as good, but only because of what Jesus has done on the cross. Father, thank you for what you've done, and continue your good work in me— giving me the right attitude as I become more and more like Jesus for your glory!

Day 7

By this time it was late in the day, so his disciples came to him. "This is a remote place," they said, "and it's already very late. Send the people away so that they can go to the surrounding countryside and villages and buy themselves something to eat." But he answered, "You give them something to eat." They said to him, "That would take more than half a year's wages! Are we to go and spend that much on bread and give it to them to eat?" "How many loaves do you have?" he asked. "Go and see." When they found out, they said, "Five—and two fish." Then Jesus directed them to have all the people sit down in groups on the green grass. So they sat down in groups of hundreds and fifties. Taking the five loaves and the two fish and looking up to heaven, he gave thanks and broke the loaves. Then he gave them to his disciples to distribute to the people. He also divided the two fish among them all. They all ate and were satisfied, and the disciples picked up twelve basketfuls of broken pieces of

bread and fish. The number of the men
who had eaten was five thousand.

MARK 6:35-44

Many of us are adept at seeing an approaching crisis
in our lives. When I see a crisis coming, my greatest
temptation is to work in my own strength and
wisdom to figure out what I need to do to stop the
event from occurring. What I see happening in the
Scriptures, however, is that each crisis becomes an
opportunity for God to reveal himself in some
way—to bring himself glory.

In the book *Experiencing God*, Henry Blackaby
points out that when Jesus's friend Lazarus was
dying, Jesus waited until Lazarus was dead to raise
him—gaining more glory for God than if he had
"simply" healed a sick person. In the feeding of the
five thousand, the opportunity for God to be
glorified was there as well—but Jesus's disciples
didn't realize it. Jesus told them the problem, and
their automatic thought was in essence to ask, "How
can we fix this problem in our own strength?" They
knew they couldn't feed this crowd, however, and
they told Jesus so.

What should our response be when we see crisis
in our lives? I want to more often remember first
who God is, how much he loves me, and ask him
what he seeks to accomplish in the situation. Then

I'll listen for as long as it takes, and I'll expect to hear what he wants me to do—things that I likely would never have come up with on my own.

God is so good that I can trust him to have actually been *waiting* to reveal himself though my troubles. I want to make this my first thought when a trial comes: that God has a new opportunity to reveal something about himself.

There's nothing better than God's solutions, as I join him in what he does for his glory.

> *Father, may your Spirit work in me*
> *that I might view problems or trials*
> *as an opportunity for you to reveal*
> *yourself—perhaps in a new way. As I*
> *face problems, please stop me from*
> *first trying to use my own*
> *intelligence to get around them. May*
> *I turn to you at all times and take*
> *part in bringing you glory!*

Day 8

They got up and returned at once to
Jerusalem. There they found the Eleven
and those with them, assembled together
and saying, "It is true! The Lord has
risen and has appeared to Simon." Then
the two told what had happened on the
way, and how Jesus was recognized by
them when he broke the bread.

LUKE 24:33-35

These two men got up and left immediately to go
back seven miles to Jerusalem from Emmaus after
Jesus had appeared to them, then disappeared. It
was almost dark, but any concerns about safety,
convention, or comfort became subservient to the
awesome news: *Jesus is alive!*

Can we somehow work this attitude into our
daily lives? I want to.

I want to live daily in the reality that Jesus is
alive. He has changed all of life for us. No longer is
there any more exciting news than this: He has done
it; he has done what no one else could do! Jesus has
brought us to God, and God has confirmed this by
raising him from the dead. I want to tell people this,

to live this, and to worship in knowing this. It's exciting news. It's stuff you don't hear happening every day, and stuff that still brings God glory.

Everyone needs to hear the news!

Lord keep me alive in the excitement of the Good News! In the midst of life's distractions, keep me focused on the reality that you're alive. Help me see things from your perspective and trust that you're always with me as a source of protection and strength. Overfill me with joy that pours out onto others. Send me out to tell everyone what you've done for your glory.

Day 9

In the morning, LORD, you hear my
voice; in the morning I lay my requests
before you and wait expectantly.

PSALM 5:3

Wait for the LORD; be strong and take
heart and wait for the LORD.

PSALM 27:14

"But when all goes well with you,
remember me and show me kindness;
mention me to Pharaoh and get me out
of this prison."… The chief cupbearer,
however, did not remember Joseph; he
forgot him. When two full years had
passed…

GENESIS 40:14; 40:23–41:1

It's so hard for me to wait. However, I know that
God uses my waiting time to work in me and in
others so that everything happens at the right time
for his glory. Do I need to try and control
everything? Do I really need to always be "doing"?
How much more do I need to see what God does, so
that he can be glorified!

I've felt for some time that I'm waiting to see God fully use the gifts he has given me. The years up until now have included so much training and preparation—so much growing. I've certainly seen God work and use me multiple times in the past, and in those times I'm so glad I waited for him. Now, once again, I'm in a place where I wonder how much longer I'll wait before walking into the next things he has prepared.

Is waiting inactive? Not at all! It's as active and productive as can be. After all, as I agree to wait, I'm being changed and prepared. I've found that I need to be ready to take the next step, because when a God-given direction comes, I must act quickly. I want to be sure I've finished the work I've been given for right now so I take time in prayer and get reminded of the last things God said. I also ask him if there's anything additional I need to do.

I experience prayer as some of the hardest but most productive work there is. It's comforting to know that while I'm waiting for the culmination of what's being prepared, God is *doing*.

There was a time when I was waiting on God's promise to provide funding for me to attend Bible school. As I prayed, the only additional thing he told me to do was to call a ministry leader at our church to sign up for a difficult teaching ministry for inner-city kids. I left a message saying my wife and I would be willing to serve in that way. It seemed completely unrelated to Bible school, but I'll mention later how it worked out as a part of God's plan for the situation.

The main thing I try to avoid is to make the waiting end prematurely. I have to let the waiting do its work. Though waiting is difficult, I know it's a sign God loves me and wants me to be ready. The moment to finally act and see the fulfillment of what God has prepared in the waiting often lasts…well, only a moment. The waiting, however, is when I and others are changed and prepared to be able to see God's hand in what's ultimately accomplished. He's so wise, and he deserves all praise and glory.

Father, please help me to wait. So often I cry out against it. It's a difficult process, but I thank you that you change me as well as set the stage for others to see you in these times. Prepare me for when the waiting is done, and bring yourself glory!

Day 10

You know how to interpret the
appearance of the sky, but you cannot
interpret the signs of the times.

MATTHEW 16:3

In some ways we know so much. We know how to
see and interpret many things in the world. But how
well do we know what God is doing today? Are we
watching for where he might be working? Are we
praying and then looking for the answer, or do we
immediately forget what we prayed and move on to
watch the news or read a book?

I need to get better at studying God's ways. I
need to watch for what he's doing in response to the
prayers of my community. I need to ask him what
he's up to, and listen for the answer. There's no one
more important than God, and there's no work more
important than his work. He's revealing himself
through what he's doing, and I don't want myself or
anyone to miss it.

Lord, keep calling me back to you.
The world has so much information
to offer, but help me notice you first

– so I'll know what you're doing
better than I know anything else.
Help me have a part in bringing you
glory, as I see what you're doing and
get involved right where you are.

Day 11

I strike a blow to my body and make it
my slave.

1 CORINTHIANS 9:27

Self-help is no help at all.

MATTHEW 16:24, The Message

For this people's heart has become
calloused; they hardly hear with their
ears, and they have closed their eyes.
Otherwise they might see with their
eyes, hear with their ears, understand
with their hearts and turn, and I would
heal them.

MATTHEW 13:15

God has given us power within ourselves to do only
one thing: turn ourselves. With every choice we
make, we choose to turn toward him or away from
him.

In our spiritual development, this is especially
important to remember. When we choose to focus
our willpower on changing ourselves, we're turning
away from God to follow the illusion that we have

36

power within ourselves to effect change. Things that seem like good goals in themselves—losing weight, eating right, acting nicer—can be our most potent distractors. These things cause us to focus on ourselves. Many of the world's religions will focus on these types of things.

When Christ shows us that we've been deceiving ourselves and that we're powerless to change, we must choose to use our willpower to turn ourselves to God—to yield ourselves to him. Then God begins to work in us, and we yield our will again as we say, "Yes, Lord, come change me."

This turning to him is hard work! We have true power to make our stubborn flesh turn to God; we must not use up our energy trying to change ourselves.

As he works in us, God continually invites us to agree with what he's doing. In this way we work what he's doing into our lives. We may end up doing some of the very things we could have focused on without him—only now his power is at work in us, since we turned to him first.

May God get the glory for empowering us with the choice to turn to him.

> *Father, there are so many apparently*
> *good things the Christian is asked to*
> *do, so many standards of appearance*

to live up to. Keep us from getting distracted and putting energy into changing ourselves—energy that's needed for the most difficult work of yielding to you. Keep our focus on you rather than on our outward performance. Thank you for giving everyone on earth the power to choose you. Thank you for making the way to intimacy with yourself through Jesus. May your Spirit continue to teach us as we say, "Yes, Lord." Receive glory as you change us by your power alone. Amen.

Day 12

Do not store up for yourselves treasures
on earth, where moths and vermin
destroy, and where thieves break in and
steal. But store up for yourselves
treasures in heaven, where moths and
vermin do not destroy, and where
thieves do not break in and steal.

MATTHEW 6:19-20

Do not be afraid of those who kill the
body but cannot kill the soul. Rather, be
afraid of the One who can destroy both
soul and body in hell.

MATTHEW 10:28

God is calling us not to suppress our desires but to
turn them toward himself. Often I get the sense that
the Christian culture where I live goes the easy
route of saying, "Stop having that desire!" instead
of asking, "How can that desire be used for the
glory of God?" Jesus doesn't just say "Stop"; rather,
he tells us where to place our desires. He's not
saying to let go of desires (as in Buddhism); rather
he's saying to turn our desires toward right things—
to have even greater desires.

For example, our desire for intimacy can be corrupted so that we willingly give ourselves over to empty or harmful relationships. God, however, is inviting us and giving us power to connect deeply with himself—to direct our desire for intimacy toward him. Nothing is better. God is inviting us into what's best, not keeping us from what's best.

C. S. Lewis wrote this widely quoted statement: "Our Lord finds our desires not too strong, but too weak. We are half-hearted creatures, fooling about with drink and sex and ambition when infinite joy is offered us, like an ignorant child who wants to go on making mud pies in a slum because he cannot imagine what is meant by the offer of a holiday at the sea. We are far too easily pleased."

How hard it can be for me to rightly direct my desires! I have to give up control and let God show me how, and show me all that I've been missing. That process can be so difficult. I must remember that my natural, sin-tainted desires are for things that are shadows of the real things—the things that fulfill me.

God loves me deeply, and he wants me to be fulfilled and made whole for his glory.

Lord, work in me so that I'll seek
only what brings you glory—the
things that are deeply fulfilling.
Make me deaf to the message that

desires must be suppressed, and instead show me how to direct my desires rightly. Thank you for the joy and freedom you bring to our lives. Receive glory as you change me, and as my desires are fulfilled by you!

Day 13

"How long will you waver between two opinions? If the LORD is God, follow him; but if Baal is God, follow him." But the people said nothing.

1 KINGS 18:21

"Answer me, LORD, answer me, so these people will know that you, LORD, are God, and that you are turning their hearts back again." Then the fire of the LORD fell and burned up the sacrifice, the wood, the stones and the soil, and also licked up the water in the trench. When all the people saw this, they fell prostrate and cried, "The LORD —he is God! The LORD —he is God!"

1 KINGS 18:37-39

Do we believe this encounter recorded in 1 Kings 18 really happened? God powerfully showed himself, and the other gods the people had worshiped did nothing.

Who do we find we're really serving: ourselves, others, or God? Are you wavering between two opinions?

I frequently need to be reminded that God is powerful over everything I face. There's no one else like him. I need to remember who he is and to serve him wholeheartedly. I'm being pushed to change by other powers around me, such as peer pressure, powerful people, or so-called experts. But in the midst of them all, there's no other God but the Lord.

He's on our side—we need to be on his.

He is for us—we need to live for him.

Father, constantly remind me of your power and wisdom. Help me remember you and your deeds at all times. By your Spirit, help me trust in you above all else, for your glory and my joy. Amen.

Day 14

Elijah was a human being, even as we are. He prayed earnestly that it would not rain, and it did not rain on the land for three and a half years.

JAMES 5:17

In your relationships with one another, have the same mindset as Christ Jesus: Who, being in very nature God, did not consider equality with God something to be used to his own advantage, rather, he made himself nothing by taking the very nature of a servant, being made in human likeness.

PHILIPPIANS 2:5-7

But when he, the Spirit of truth, comes, he will guide you into all the truth. He will not speak on his own; he will speak only what he hears, and he will tell you what is yet to come. He will glorify me because it is from me that he will receive what he will make known to you.

JOHN 16:13-14

I've heard people debate about whether Jesus gave up his power as God when he came to earth. I used to think that if we viewed Jesus as a kind of superman (who therefore didn't need to depend on the Father for everything), we might conclude that we don't have the same power Christ had. Now, I see that it probably doesn't matter. Whether we think Christ modeled dependence on the power of the Father, or that Christ showed his own power and divinity (or some of both), the important thing is that we understand that God's power is 100 percent available to us for doing his will on earth. We depend on the Father, and we have the same power available to us that raised Christ from death. Jesus lives in us, and his Spirit empowers us.

We must not think—when we look at Christ— that the things he did are impossible for us. Anyone who serves the Lord of all has the power to do everything God wants done. It doesn't depend upon who we are, but on who God is. The only limit to what we can do is the boundary of the purpose God has for our lives. Some people are made to do one thing and some another—all for the great glory of God.

> *Lord, help me not to look at my own*
> *strength, power, or charisma when I*
> *consider what I can do; instead, help*
> *me look to Christ as the example of*
> *what's possible for any Christian, if*

45

you so will. Guide me and each of us into the works you've planned for us to do. Help us work together as we do our part—you have made us into one body. Give us faith in your ability as we see our own shortcomings. Receive all the glory as your power—not our own—is clearly shown for the entire world to see!

Day 15

Ask me and I will tell you remarkable
secrets you do not know about things to
come.

JEREMIAH 33:3, NLT

Why do I not ask God enough? Am I so afraid, so
doubtful of his power, so unlike him in my desires?
In the verse above, God tells Jeremiah to simply ask
him, and he will reveal remarkable secrets. He'll
reveal things as yet unknown. Why? God does this
for his glory.

I believe we, like Jeremiah, also have an
invitation to ask God. God has a set purpose for
each of our lives. Jeremiah was a prophet; what are
you? Are you called like Jeremiah to speak a word
or live out a message for your church? Are you
called to communicate the gospel? Are you called to
teach others? Whatever it is, it will take God, his
power, and his revelation so you can be used for his
glory.

Ask him, talk to him about whatever is on your
heart. He's just waiting for you to ask!

Father, how good it is that you desire interaction with us! Help me depend on you out of sincere belief in your power and love. Tell me remarkable things, and delight in my joy. Keep calling me back to you again and again. I need you, Lord. Receive great glory as you reveal your plans and empower me for service in your name.

Day 16

I rejoice in following your statutes as
one rejoices in great riches.

PSALM 119:14

Some people may think of following God as
something awful—a "discipline" for the committed.
It can feel awful, I suppose, but not for the reasons
someone might expect. Living God's way fights
against my corrupted desires. I'm going through the
process of being made into the person that I would
have been if there was no sin in me or in the
world—but that process isn't complete.

As the old life in me dies, it can be painful. But
God's Spirit is at the same time giving me the desire
for this new life. Even as I read the passage above
from Psalm 119, I can feel the joy of God. Through
his work in me, I'm growing in having the same
kind of zeal for following him that I could have for
great riches. He is a remarkable treasure worthy of
being pursued, and my joy overflows as I do so. I'm
excited to keep living in his way, as he makes me to
be like Jesus for his own glory.

Lord, thank you for what you're doing in me. Give me a desire for you that goes beyond anything. Give me a hunger for your Scriptures. May your Holy Spirit bring them to life. Keep on making me become the person I'll be when you've restored all things—indeed, you've promised to do this. Help me pursue you all my days, and thank you again for bringing yourself glory.

Day 17

For this world in its present form is
passing away.

1 CORINTHIANS 7:31

Wait! Oh, you mean this world is not our home?
You really mean it? And you're saying it's not that I
have to try harder to deny my comfort, but that I
have to understand and experience where a better
comfort lies? One that's more stable and fulfilling?

As I walk with Christ, I'm finally realizing what
my future home is. It's not some ethereal place, but
a real earth, a fully sanctified creation of God. It's a
place more tangible than this one, where I'll be even
more deeply connected to God. This frees me from
the "comfort versus mission" struggle. I can spend
my life freely for God and his mission because I
have this wonderful home coming. It's as real as the
dirt I walk on.

God is calling people to himself, and he wants
me to join in the work of sacrificial love.

Sacrifice doesn't mean I have to try harder to
deny myself the pleasures of this world. In serving
God, I'm simply ignoring the idea that this world is

all there is; instead I'm focusing on what's to come. I focus on how what's done now impacts that world. I look forward to getting far more than I give up as I keep busy with "kingdom work."

It's so freeing and fulfilling to be useful for God. For his glory, I look forward to a coming world that's real—where we'll all see the fulfillment of what he has begun in us here and now.

> *Lord, help me even now to enjoy the future you have for us. Take my eyes off this world and its unfulfilling, enslaving pleasures. Keep me alive and moving in mission—knowing that everything is promised us, and we won't miss out on a thing. Be glorified though me as I joyfully live in the promise of a new world!*

Day 18

But seek first his kingdom and his
righteousness, and all these things will
be given to you as well.

MATTHEW 6:33

I believe Jesus's message is basically this: we can't
concern ourselves with both our life and God's
kingdom; we have to choose one or the other.

In a book on management I read recently, Mark
McCormack wrote about the inefficiency of more
than one manager in a company "worrying" about
how to solve the same problem. Another writer,
A. J. Jacobs, tells of outsourcing his worry to his
personal assistant in India. He says this worked—
someone else was worrying about his problems, and
he didn't feel a need to! In the same way, if God
promises to take care of our lives, we can be busy
taking care of something else. So what exactly
should we be doing?

After my wife and I had been married for half a
year, we packed our belongings into our red Geo
Metro and headed toward the next place God would
reveal for us to serve at. After meeting with a
couple other churches, we ended up connecting with

an amazing community that was also close to a Bible college we knew of. The Lord made it clear that he wanted us to move onto campus and for me to enroll in a Bible and music program there, but that we should wait on him alone for the finances (in order to reveal something about God to those watching us).

The deadline for payment soon came, and we had no money. We were given one day to move off campus.

The following day, twenty minutes before the finance office closed, the Lord used a phone message I made at least a week earlier (see Day 9) to connect us with a woman in her nineties who had a heart for people learning the Bible. Each quarter after that, I would again cry out to God to take care of the bill, and this same benefactor would "randomly" show up at our church and want to supply the funds. I don't know that I saw her show up at any other time—I believe it was getting difficult for her to make the trip to the church she'd been a member of for over eighty years.

As we put the Lord's plan first, he provided for our needs through this benefactor, as well as through two jobs on campus for my wife. Students and leaders at the school as well as local city ministry leaders in our church got to see God at work, the God who still provides today. It wouldn't have been possible to be God's witnesses in that way if we were trying to provide in our own strength.

God has freed us up to minister—to live for him rather than for fear and self. He frees us to set our minds on his kingdom goals. He has things that he has prepared for us to do, so let's be busy being his witnesses—his ambassadors—wherever we are. Let's encourage beauty in the world by bringing Christ to the nations. Let's not get slowed down by trying to do God's job of figuring out how our needs will be taken care of. He has so many people that he wants to be known by. If we'll let God take care of us, we can truly take care of seeking him first with joyful hearts, and bring him glory.

Father, help us to seek your priorities for this world before anything else. Help us trust that you've freed us to do so. Thank you for providing all we need as we joyfully serve you. What a life you offer us! Thank you, and we pray that you'll receive great glory. Amen.

Day 19

Now Elisha had said to the woman whose son he had restored to life, "Go away with your family and stay for a while wherever you can, because the LORD has decreed a famine in the land that will last seven years." The woman proceeded to do as the man of God said. She and her family went away and stayed in the land of the Philistines seven years. At the end of the seven years she came back from the land of the Philistines and went to appeal to the king for her house and land. The king was talking to Gehazi, the servant of the man of God, and had said, "Tell me about all the great things Elisha has done." Just as Gehazi was telling the king how Elisha had restored the dead to life, the woman whose son Elisha had brought back to life came to appeal to the king for her house and land. Gehazi said, "This is the woman, my lord the king, and this is her son whom Elisha restored to life." The king asked the woman about it, and she told him. Then he assigned an official to her case and said to him, "Give back everything that

belonged to her, including all the
income from her land from the day she
left the country until now."

2 KINGS 8:1-6

It's wonderful how God can do anything, and how
he even cares enough to prepare the way for us.
This woman in 2 Kings 8 did what Elisha said,
apparently without worrying that her house and
lands would be lost. She'd previously seen God's
power at work in restoring her son to life. When she
returns to beg the king to give her the house and
land rightfully belonging to her, the conversation
taking place when she arrives is already about her.

We can move forward in doing the Lord's
will—knowing that he's already preparing the way
for us.

Yesterday I mentioned how the Lord prepared
the way for my wife and me when we needed him
to provide money for Bible college and housing.
The woman he used had a passion for giving money
for people to learn the Bible, and was sponsoring a
student whom we would be teaching as part of an
inner-city ministry. And since she and her husband
had lived next to the college at its former location
thirty years before, she was already familiar with it.
The afternoon we talked with her, she was
immediately ready to write a check. Miraculously, it

came in the mail the next day. This made us laugh, because our mail to the college was typically delayed longer than mail to anywhere else nearby; we don't even know how she got it into that day's mail (since we spoke with her somewhat late in the day).

Don't be afraid to do what God asks—to go where he leads. He will take care of you. He's even now preparing the way for you, and he will gain glory.

Lord, help us trust you—and to remember that you're in control and that you love us so much! Thank you for preparing the way for us and for glorifying yourself as you aid us. You are a good God!

Day 20

He had no beauty or majesty to attract
us to him, nothing in his appearance that
we should desire him.

ISAIAH 53:2

Beware of what looks good. I'm often in danger of confusing a good deal or circumstance with God's will. And it's just as easy for me to interpret a high price or bad circumstance as a sign that God isn't in something. Such judgments, which are based on a surface level of sight, do not in themselves reveal God's desires and plans. We must stay connected to God through his Spirit living in us. In this way we can know the heart of God and begin to see as he sees.

Many people missed what God was doing through Jesus because of Jesus's appearance—the way he did things, and how he looked as he died a shameful death. In the church, I've served on hiring committees where the temptation was to judge people by their external qualifications alone. However, I think of David—not many would have hired him to be the king of Israel, but God saw his heart.

I think it likely that there are many today with hearts fixed on God, able to do whatever he wants to empower them to do, because they trust in him. Do I notice them when we meet? I don't want to miss seeing God at work—either through people or in situations—because I'm not watching with God's eyes. I want to stay so deeply connected to him that I'll know his heart and take part in revealing his glory.

Father, keep drawing me to yourself that I might see this world as you see it. May I be led by your Spirit alone as I make decisions about people and things. Help me join you in your work. I'm so excited that you know how to bring yourself glory!

Day 21

So in Christ Jesus you are all children of
God through faith, for all of you who
were baptized into Christ have clothed
yourselves with Christ. There is neither
Jew nor Gentile, neither slave nor free,
nor is there male and female, for you are
all one in Christ Jesus. If you belong to
Christ, then you are Abraham's seed,
and heirs according to the promise.

GALATIANS 3:26-29

Were you a slave when you were called?
Don't let it trouble you—although if you
can gain your freedom, do so. For the
one who was a slave when called to
faith in the Lord is the Lord's freed
person; similarly, the one who was free
when called is Christ's slave. You were
bought at a price; do not become slaves
of human beings. Brothers and sisters,
each person, as responsible to God,
should remain in the situation they were
in when God called them.

1 CORINTHIANS 7:21-24

Wives, in the same way submit
yourselves to your own husbands so

that, if any of them do not believe the
word, they may be won over without
words by the behavior of their wives,
when they see the purity and reverence
of your lives.

1 PETER 3:1-2

I constantly feel the world pulling me toward seeing
a person's role or job as tied to their value.
However, our value in God's eyes doesn't change,
nor does it depend on anything we do.

I enjoyed working as a janitor for over twenty
years, and it was interesting to me that when my job
came up in conversation, people didn't seem to
think I was very important—not as important as
when I later worked as a musician or
telecommunications technician. Another result of
this tie between value and job is that people feel
devalued when they aren't allowed to perform a
certain role even though they might be qualified for
it.

God reveals himself mightily in the love we
show people in the midst of hate, oppression, and
mistrust. And the Lord even uses broken things and
systems in the world to change us—to make us
more like him. What I do in life should come out of
the gifts God has given me *and* the calling on my
life. If I get caught up in striving to do certain jobs

in order to increase my value in the eyes of others, I'm likely forgetting that my value is handed me by God. My value is the same as a child of the God of the universe, whether I'm a pastor or janitor, whether I'm a leader or a follower.

We each have a call on our lives, and each of us should fulfill that call within whatever life context we find ourselves. God primarily wants us to grow to be like Christ and to help others to do so as well. We do this through love, through submission, at times through suffering. Through it all, we're deeply loved, accepted, and valued so much that Jesus died for us. God has ways of gaining glory that are unexpected, and in the end we'll all be shown to be his.

Lord, help us submit to you in the midst of a culture that puts so much emphasis on our value being linked to our job or role in life. Help us submit to one another in whatever way you lead, so that we can take part in something greater—lives being changed. May we get all our affirmation from you so that we no longer have any taste for the affirmation of the world. Make us true servants—all for your great glory.

Day 22

Why not rather be wronged? Why not
rather be cheated?

1 CORINTHIANS 6:7

Do not say, "I'll pay you back for this
wrong!" Wait for the LORD, and he will
avenge you.

PROVERBS 20:22

Human anger does not produce the
righteousness that God desires.

JAMES 1:20

How much time and energy do we spend on
protecting ourselves? How much of our day goes
into making sure we obtain all our rights?

What's best for others and for God's glory
doesn't always include getting what I think I
deserve. Often I must set myself aside for the sake
of others. This presupposes that I'm connected to
the source of strength—the Spirit of God in Christ.
As I put myself aside, God makes sure justice is
served.

I have the most trouble in this area when I'm cheated financially. A few years back, I paid for a one-year membership to an organization that would help me with song publishing. The next morning I found out they had misrepresented themselves, and that there was also no way to recover my fee. At other times I've been mistakenly overcharged for an item, or contractors have damaged something I own. God has been helping me to simply let these sorts of things go when it's a better witness to do so. He'll take care of me in spite of the lies or mistakes of others.

I'm not saying we'll never be called to speak out or take action—only that if we do so, it shouldn't be from a desire to make things even.

There's great freedom when we can truly put ourselves in the hands of God, just as Jesus "entrusted himself to him who judges justly" (1 Peter 2:23). No longer do we have to fight for ourselves. God is fighting for us; he will repay. He'll take care of the liar and the cheater, and he'll continue to provide for us even when others make mistakes at our expense. We can put our energies into loving our neighbor, our brother or sister, and even our enemy. If God does have us act, it will be out of love and on his behalf, not our own. If he doesn't call us to act outwardly, we can pray for those involved.

Finally, if we really need justice, it's much better for God (who's far bigger than I am) to be the one taking care of it. And the most wonderful thing is that he can give people an opportunity to repent unlike anything we're able to accomplish ourselves. This is the chance he has given all of us who've turned to him. The character of the God who loved us even while we were his enemies will be revealed through us to the world—all for his glory!

Father, when I'm wronged by others, help me remember that you're in charge. Help me continue to act out of love. And when I cannot affect others, continue to take charge of doing whatever is needed to set things right. May I fully know your love for me so that I might fully love all people. Help me remember everything you've given to me that I didn't deserve. Guide me in all things. You are good to us, God – be glorified as I remember this!

Day 23

Do not let Hezekiah persuade you to
trust in the LORD when he says, "The
LORD will surely deliver us; this city
will not be given into the hand of the
king of Assyria." Do not listen to
Hezekiah. This is what the king of
Assyria says: Make peace with me and
come out to me. Then each of you will
eat fruit from your own vine and fig tree
and drink water from your own cistern,
until I come and take you to a land like
your own—a land of grain and new
wine, a land of bread and vineyards, a
land of olive trees and honey. Choose
life and not death!

2 KINGS 18:30-33

If I put myself in the position of the people hearing
the Assyrian king's words in 2 Kings 18, I find it's
similar to the kinds of choices I think we all face
quite often. We know the promise of the Lord to
take care of us, yet very tangible problems present
themselves to us. Can we really "just have faith," as
little children do?

In this Scripture passage, these people faced an undefeated enemy. They risked losing their lives if God wasn't real—if he's not who he said he was. When I'm in this kind of situation, I can almost always see the way out—I've been educated on how I can take things into my own hands and resolve the situation. Although it brings little glory to God if I take my own way out, it's very tempting for me to do so.

Everyone hearing the king of Assyria's promises of nice things if they surrendered was probably tempted as well. Still, in this situation, the people trusted in God to deliver them.

So far, my family and I have moved seven times without a job promise—we had only direction from God and his promise to provide. Each time, I've known I was in a situation where if God doesn't exist, everything would fall apart. This has been hard, but it has been a blessing for me and others to see God do exactly as he promised each time.

Hezekiah prayed to the Lord—laid out the situation—and the prophet Isaiah foretold God's response (in 2 Kings 19). Things happened just as the prophet said. After the angel of the Lord killed 185,000 soldiers in the enemy camp, King Sennacherib of Assyria returned home and was killed by two of his sons.

Who is God? A God who cares for his people and keeps his promises! He's a God who has very real solutions for very real problems. He'll keep his promises to you, and get glory for himself in the process.

Help us to trust you, Lord. May you be so real and so well known to us that we cannot help but trust you in all situations. When we're tested, lead us to yourself, for your great glory. Amen.

Day 24

"As surely as the LORD your God lives,"
she replied, "I don't have any bread—
only a handful of flour in a jar and a
little oil in a jug. I am gathering a few
sticks to take home and make a meal for
myself and my son, that we may eat it—
and die." Elijah said to her, "Don't be
afraid. Go home and do as you have
said. But first make a small loaf of bread
for me from what you have and bring it
to me, and then make something for
yourself and your son. For this is what
the LORD, the God of Israel, says: 'The
jar of flour will not be used up and the
jug of oil will not run dry until the day
the LORD sends rain on the land.'"

1 KINGS 17:12-14

God can sustain us; he can take care of us. I want to
be sure to give at all times, to be generous with
others. In 1 Kings 17, a widow gave her last bit of
food for Elijah—having only his word that the Lord
will provide. We can give our final resources to
God as well—knowing he cares for us.

I love the story in Mark 12 where Jesus spoke to his disciples about the widow who gave her last two coins as an offering. She must have been trusting in God, because Jesus said she gave all she had to live on. We shouldn't think that if we have very little money, time, or other resources, then we cannot give. Likewise we shouldn't think that God doesn't notice when our hearts are devoted to him.

I've heard criticism toward people whose giving to God's work is disproportionate to their income (not leaving enough for themselves). I think, however, that the Lord loves our faith. He loves our knowing that he wants our hearts to be his and that he provides for us. (I'm speaking here only of giving what we actually have—not necessarily about going into debt, which would be giving other people's money.)

There are always others with needs nearby, and God is inviting you and me to be involved with him in meeting those needs. As we do so, they and we will get to know God intimately as our provider, and he will be glorified.

> *Father help us trust you at all times*
> *for everything. You so wonderfully*
> *provide for us, and we ask you to use*
> *us in our plenty or in our want. Even*
> *in seasons of drought—where things*
> *might not get better for some time—*

may we bless others, see you at work, and bring you glory!

Day 25

Trust in the Lord with all your heart and
lean not on your own understanding; in
all your ways submit to him, and he will
make your paths straight.

PROVERBS 3:5-6

When the Lord encourages me to do something, I don't expect to immediately understand it. God seems to tell me the "what," but almost never the "why." This forces me to trust him more—I cannot lean on my own understanding. I seek to follow him and acknowledge him, and he has always made things in my life work out for his glory.

In fact, looking back, this is almost always the answer to the "why" question: he's gaining glory in the eyes of others. It's hard to believe I get so worked up about not knowing the "why," since I know that each time I get the blessing of being used by him and seeing him at work.

I've mentioned before how my wife and I, in our first year of marriage, felt our first call to move from where we were located in order to see where we would serve next in ministry. At about the same time, three new "doors" of opportunity were opening up for me if I chose to stay where I was. At the place where I had been working, a new position was offered that seemed a perfect fit for me both in the type of work and the schedule. Two ministry organizations nearby were also interested in having me serve with them. It was very difficult for me to turn them down and follow God's call to move out of state, because the opportunities looked so good!

We traveled, visiting and praying with people from two other wonderful ministries. But the Lord inexplicably still seemed to be urging us onward. Finally, during a brief visit to a church that a friend of ours was at (a visit that I almost canceled twice that day due to obstacles), the Lord finally made it clear that this was where we were to serve. It wasn't even a place where we or they had any plans for our doing ministry.

As we gave to that church, and as I later served on staff in various positions, it provided for us for many years. We saw many people come to know God more deeply, and we ourselves grew in him. It was an absolutely essential time of learning how to use our gifts and how to open up our lives so people could see God at work. He brought himself glory in ways I could never have foreseen.

God's thoughts truly are higher and greater than my own. He can see things in a much broader way than I can. And he alone has power to do anything. I want to trust him at all times because he has the big picture. I don't want to lean on my own understanding—I want to follow him and acknowledge his greatness.

All praise, honor, and glory to our all-knowing, all-powerful God!

> *May I follow you, Lord, even when you don't tell me why. Help me not to make an idol of my own thoughts and understanding. May I always acknowledge you—both before and after you show that you were in control all along. You'll always know more than I do, so help me follow you, for your glory.*

Day 26

Therefore do not let anyone judge you
by what you eat or drink, or with regard
to a religious festival, a New Moon
celebration or a Sabbath day. These are
a shadow of the things that were to
come; the reality, however, is found in
Christ.

COLOSSIANS 2:16-17

Do we truly realize that Christ has fulfilled the law? Whatever we do now is not for our salvation but rather out of love for the Lord and our brother or sister.

Furthermore, we shine God's light to the nations and show ourselves holy as we're led by the Spirit of Christ. We need not observe any special days or rules—these have been "observed" for all time by Christ on our behalf.

I admit it's confusing when we read something in the Old Testament similar to "this will remain an observance before the Lord for all time—it shall never be rescinded." But it hasn't been rescinded—it has been *fulfilled* for all time by Jesus. In the same way that Christ is the King in David's line who rules for all time, he's also the High Priest who offered himself one time for all who trust in his power to save.

So observe whatever days or rules you want—whatever helps you to stay close to the Lord and to bless other people. Just remember that others may not make the same observance, and they don't need to.

May God be glorified by how we love one another, now that we're free from judgment and condemnation and bound to Christ.

> *Father, help us so that we now turn in all things to the Ruler rather than the rules. May we live in him and he in us—in Christ who has fully met all the requirements of the law. Just the same, may we refrain from judging others who use observances to draw close to you, and may we be just as free from feeling constrained by the judgment of others. Keep us in Christ, so that through this relationship we'll bring you glory.*

Day 27

You know that you will receive an
inheritance from the Lord as a reward. It
is the Lord Christ you are serving.

COLOSSIANS 3:24

How sad we may think it is. The life of a man
comes to an end. He has no wealth. No one will
remember who he was.

Yet this man faithfully served the Lord in all he
did. He had a wisdom that saw beyond death—
beyond this life alone. He worked hard—spending
all his waking energy on serving the Lord by
serving others. He brought the Lord glory here on
earth. Furthermore, he hasn't missed out on
anything in spending his life in this way. He has a
reward that's greater than we can imagine. It will
last not twenty years, not thirty, not one hundred,
but for eternity.

So please encourage me in my own walk with
the Lord by letting me see you invest in eternal
things like this man. Let's begin to change our
culture's perspective on what a long-term
investment is. It can be important to make financial
investments here on earth, but it depends on their

purpose and the purpose God has for our lives. He may want you or me to give a dollar to someone today instead of two dollars tomorrow. He may want us to give time to someone even though we have a different plan for our day.

He wants true, long-term investing—and we have a guaranteed return. Let's do our best to stay connected to him, asking what eternal investing looks like for us, and bring him great glory.

How wonderful you are, Lord God!
Guide us in the use of our time and
finances that we might store up
heavenly treasures. May your will be
done at all times by your people.
Help us invest wisely with an eternal
perspective. May we encourage one
another in this, for your glory.

Day 28

Father, if you are willing, take this cup
from me; yet not my will, but yours be
done.

LUKE 22:42

Be very careful, then, how you live—
not as unwise but as wise, making the
most of every opportunity, because the
days are evil. Therefore do not be
foolish, but understand what the Lord's
will is.

EPHESIANS 5:15-17

What I want is not the most important thing.

Many times, I follow God even though I'm not
so sure I agree with what he's asking. I do this
knowing that I'll come around eventually to agree
with his will.

If you're like me, there's a sort of filter that
every decision goes through: "Do I like this or not?"
It's a filter I'm slowly getting rid of, since I can see
things only in part. I cannot actually tell how I'll
feel about something later on.

What God wants is what's best for us in the long run. This applies to everything small or large in our lives. Think of the person who gives birth to a child she felt too busy for. Years later, she'll probably be so thankful for this new life. It doesn't matter what she thought before the event—her preconceived notion; it only matters what God's good plan is. And since he's able to make all things work for good in our lives, in a sense everything works out to accomplish his plan. Therefore, don't get trapped by the idea circulating all around that our will and feelings are most important in all things. Our striving to keep ourselves safe and happy will never bring us the kind of satisfaction and joy that God's will does.

All praise to God for lifting from our shoulders the burden of having to have our own way. May we joyfully do everything that pleases him, for our own future delight and for his great glory.

*Father, you know what's best for us
and for the world. Continue to lead
us, and help us say yes to everything
you want. When we don't like our
picture of what we think the future
will be, help us have faith in your
goodness, so that you will have the
glory. Amen.*

Day 29

Don't push your way to the front; don't
sweet-talk your way to the top.
Put yourself aside, and help others get
ahead. Don't be obsessed with getting
your own advantage. Forget yourselves
long enough to lend a helping hand.

PHILIPPIANS 2:3-4, The Message

I'm learning to apply this passage from Philippians
2 to the times when I buy something from an
individual. Instead of considering only how I can
get the best deal, I consider how I can bless the
person I'm buying from. I've begun to consider my
witness for Christ, to think about how people will
remember me when the transaction is done.

Now this isn't about being taken advantage of.
Feeding the corruption of people who are trying to
take advantage of us is not the best thing for them.
Each of us has to do our best—with the Spirit of
God helping us—to discern the mind and heart of
the seller. As we do this, we then release our cares
about our own welfare, knowing that God cares for
us. I ask myself, "How am I living the truth that

God takes care of my needs as I serve him? Am I being generous?"

God has sacrificed for me and for each one of us because he loves us. Let's show our love for others by being generous, and together work for his glory!

(I think there are many other ways to bring God glory in a business context as well. I encourage you to go back to the Philippians passage above, and think of two or three such ways that apply to you.)

Lord, please help me think of the needs of others above my own needs. Even during financial transactions, when we're trained to get the best deal, help me be a blessing. May the example of your self-sacrifice for my benefit drive me to sacrifice for the benefit of others. Help me remember that you provide for me, and that money is one of the tools you give me to bless others with. Receive glory from all that I do Lord!

Day 30

When they came together in Galilee, he
said to them, "The Son of Man is going
to be delivered into the hands of men.
They will kill him, and on the third day
he will be raised to life." And the
disciples were filled with grief.

MATTHEW 17:22-23

What do we hear when we read the Scriptures?
What do we see when the answer to our prayers is
in front of us along with life's trials? What do we
feel when God is working in us—growing us in the
midst of our mistakes? What do we think of who he
is? Do we expect him to really do anything great
and exciting and powerful?

He's always working, even in the midst of much
evil. With the help of the Spirit, let's work to move
our eyes from our temporary afflictions to what God
is doing to bring himself eternal glory. Watch for
him after prayer. Expect him to speak somehow as
we read the Scriptures or pray or worship. Expect
him to speak throughout the day amid whatever
we're doing—knowing that he's always present.

Look for what he's teaching us when we fail—how he's growing us to be like him.

We work these things into our lives so that if he were to tell us that he'll die and then be raised from death, we would hear the second half of the sentence and rejoice in his power.

God is always working to bring himself glory, and if we see him at work—even in the midst of everything else we could focus on—we'll rejoice continually.

> *Father, may we focus on your power*
> *and goodness at all times for your*
> *glory. May we be able to truly live*
> *your servant Paul's words: "Rejoice*
> *in the Lord always. I will say it*
> *again: Rejoice!" (Philippians 4:4).*

About the Author

COLIN CHALMERS is a musician and songwriter living near Santa Cruz, California. He feels blessed to have seen God provide in unusual ways for him and his family, and he wants to continue to stay connected with God and make people aware of His beauty.

Music: Visit
http://ForHisGloryDevo.com
for songs that go with this
devotional.

Made in the USA
San Bernardino, CA
23 June 2018